Level Four

Compiled and arranged by Wesley Schaum
CD orchestrations by Jeff Schaum

FOREWORD

This series offers students an appealing variety of musical styles in a single album: classical – jazz – patriotic – folk. A brief paragraph with background information is included for several pieces.

All books include a CD with orchestrated accompaniments. Each piece has two CD tracks: 1) Performance tempo 2) Practice tempo

The intent of the CD is to provide an incentive for practice by demonstrating how the finished piece will sound. The slower practice tempo assists the student in maintaining a steady beat, using the correct rhythm and gaining valuable ensemble experience while making practice more fun.

> A performance /practice CD is enclosed in an envelope attached to the back inside cover.

INDEX

Schaum Publications, Inc.
10235 N. Port Washington Rd. • Mequon, WI 53092
www.schaumpiano.net

Mexican Hat Dance

Mexican Folk Tune

Vivace ♩. = 92-104

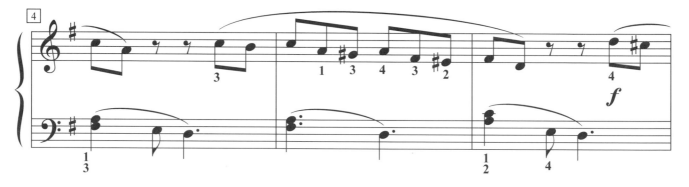

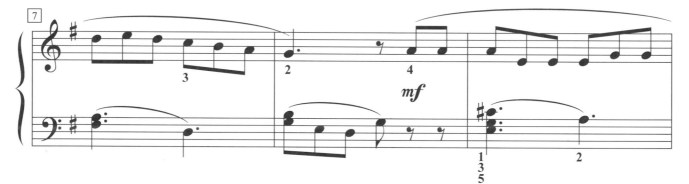

2

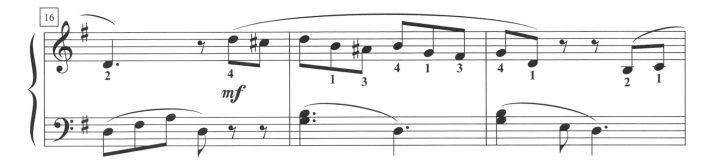

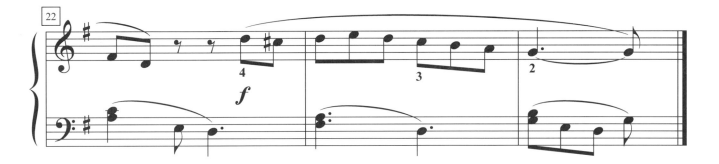

In Mexico, this tune is known as "Jarabe Tapatio" and is the national dance of Mexico. It is believed that it was first performed in the capital, Mexico City, in 1790.

Jarabe is a dance form that originated in Spain. It typically has several sections with different themes and various tempos. *Tapatio* is the name given to someone who lives in the Mexican province of Guadalajara, where the dance first became popular.

CD Track 1: Performance tempo
CD Track 2: Practice tempo (played twice)
(Each track includes two-measure introduction)

4

Minuet in F

Animato ♩ = 120-138

Wolfgang Amadeus Mozart, K2

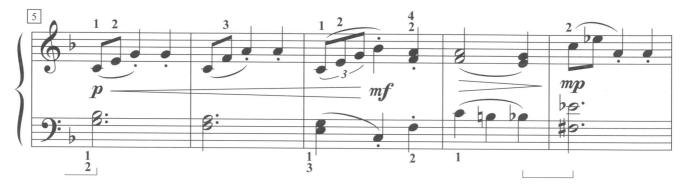

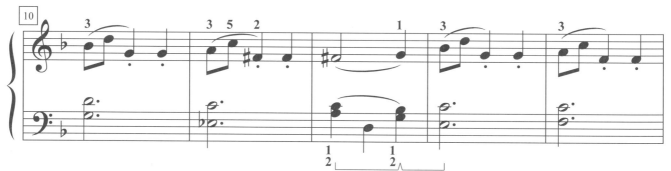

 CD Track 3: Performance tempo
CD Track 4: Practice tempo (played twice)

Hornpipe

Con brio ♩= 82-94

Irish Folk Dance

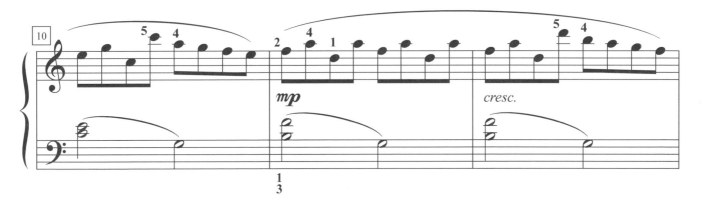

 CD Track 5: Performance tempo
CD Track 6: Practice tempo (played twice)

Carnival of Venice

Italian Folk Song

Giocoso ♩. = 56-63

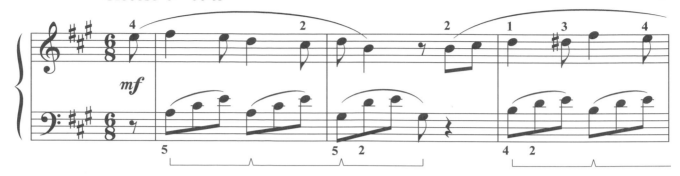

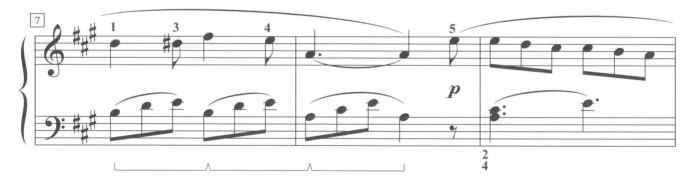

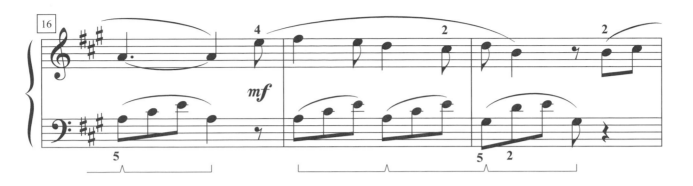

The *Carnival of Venice* is named for the city of Venice, Italy. The carnival is an exuberant celebration with many people wearing costumes and masks. The event occurs just before the beginning of Lent. *Mardi Gras* is a similar celebration in New Orleans, Louisiana.

Venice is built on dozens of islands adjoining the coast of Italy. Canals run between the islands instead of streets. Most of the islands are connected by pedestrian bridges. "Water buses," "water taxis" and barges move people and supplies through the canals. Traditional gondolas are also used.

 CD Track 7: Performance tempo
CD Track 8: Practice tempo (played twice)

American Patrol

F. W. Meacham

Allegro ♩ = 86-98

The sequence of dynamics in *American Patrol* suggests a group of soldiers approaching from a distance, passing by, and continuing on its way. The piece starts softly, gradually builds in sound, then fades away.

Frank W. Meacham was born in Buffalo, New York and later moved to Brooklyn, New York where he worked as a composer and arranger. This march was written in 1885.

CD Track 9: Performance tempo
CD Track 10: Practice tempo (played twice)

Ramblin' Swing

Vivo ♩ = 118-132 *(swing 8ths)*

Stanford King

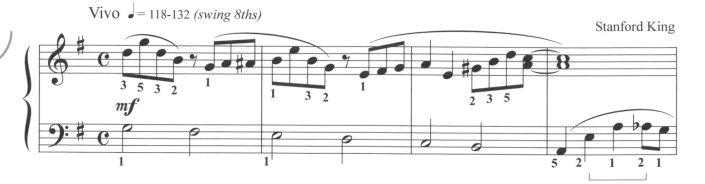

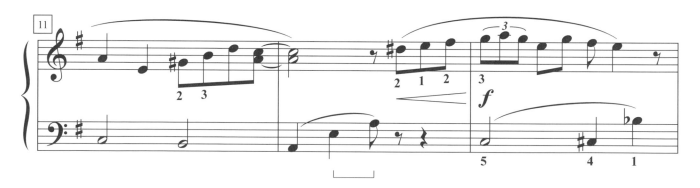

CD Track 11: Performance tempo
CD Track 12: Practice tempo (played twice)

Minuet in G

Ludwig van Beethoven

Allegretto ♩= 96-106

Fine

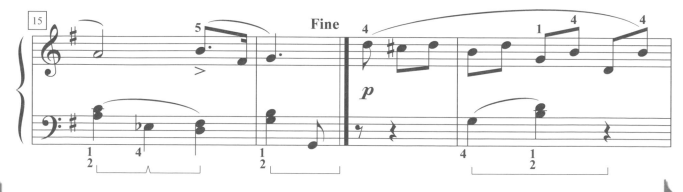

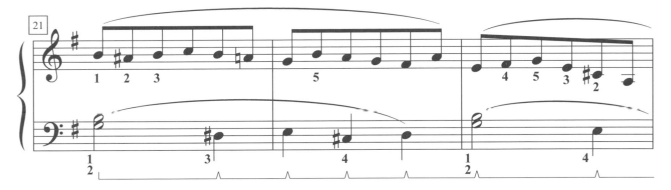

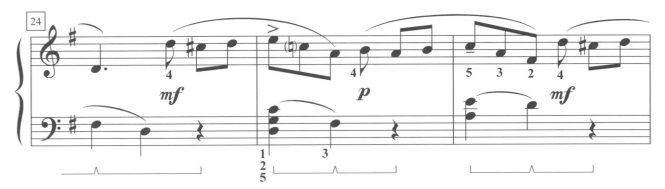

D.C. al fine

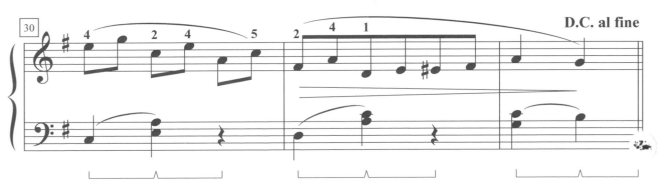

 CD Track 13: Performance tempo
CD Track 14: Practice tempo (played twice)

Dark Eyes

Allegro moderato ♪ = 126-144

Russian Gypsy Folk Song

CD Track 15: Performance tempo
CD Track 16: Practice tempo (played twice)

Square Bear

Marcato ♩ = 100-112 *(swing 8ths)*

Wesley Schaum

CD Track 17: Performance tempo
CD Track 18: Practice tempo (played twice)

Dixie

Music and lyrics by
Daniel D. Emmett

Vivace ♩ = 78-88

I___ wish I was___ in the land of cot - ton, old times there are

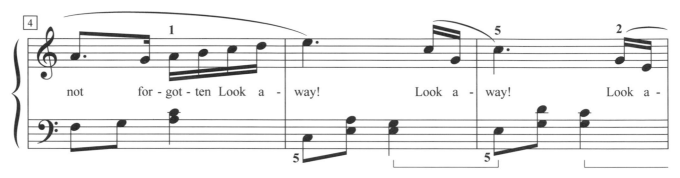

not for - got - ten Look a - way! Look a - way! Look a -

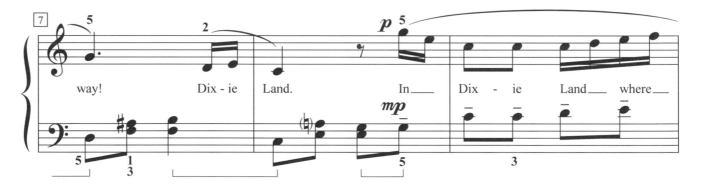

way! Dix - ie Land. In___ Dix - ie Land___ where___

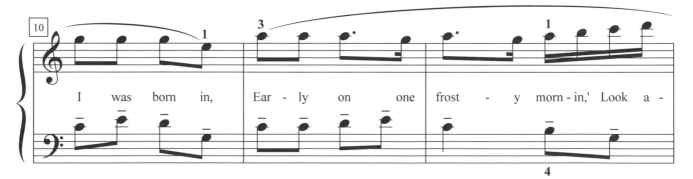

I was born in, Ear - ly on one frost - y morn - in,' Look a -

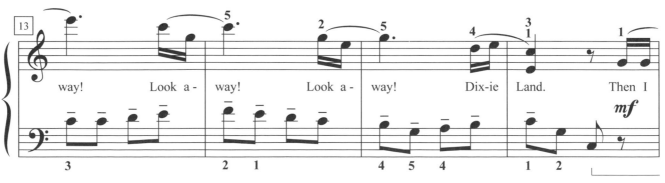

way! Look a - way! Look a - way! Dix-ie Land. Then I

CD Track 19: Performance tempo
CD Track 20: Practice tempo (played twice)

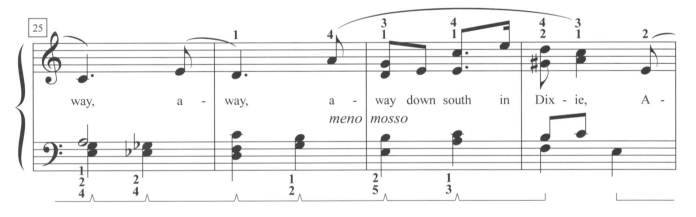

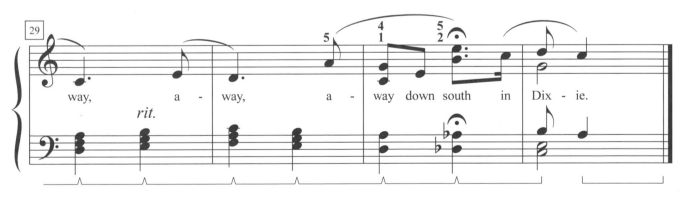

The composer, Daniel Emmett, wrote "Dixie" in 1859 for a traveling musical show. In the song, Dixie refers to the region of the southern United States, roughly from the Atlantic Ocean to states bordering the Mississippi River.

In this arrangement, notice that the melody for "Yankee Doodle" (accented notes in the left hand) is combined with "Dixie" in measures 8 through 16.

Blue Danube Waltz

Johann Strauss, Jr., Op. 314

Con eleganza ♩ = 146-158

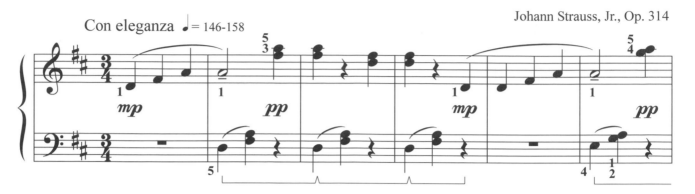

🄲🄳 **CD Track 21: Performance tempo**
CD Track 22: Practice tempo (played twice)

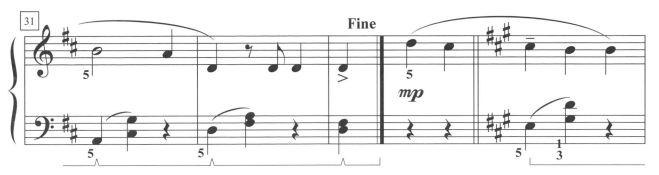

The *Blue Danube Waltz* is named for the Danube river which flows from southern Germany through Austria, Hungary and other eastern European countries.

Johann Strauss, Jr. wrote this famous waltz in 1867. It was composed for a dance hall orchestra. The original waltz is quite lengthy with ten different themes. This arrangement uses only the first two themes of the piece.

Maple Leaf Rag

Energico ♩ = 116-132

Scott Joplin

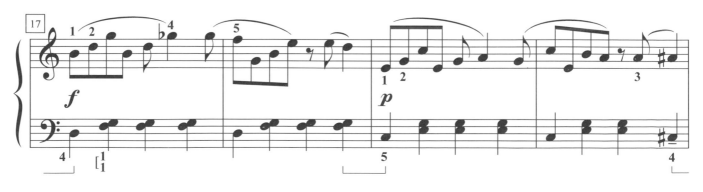

CD Track 23: Performance tempo
CD Track 24: Practice tempo (played twice)

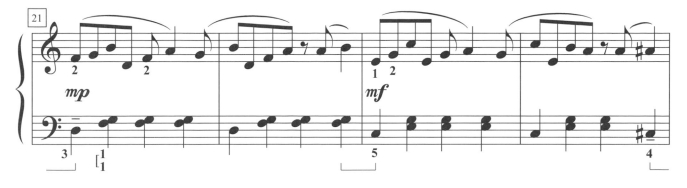

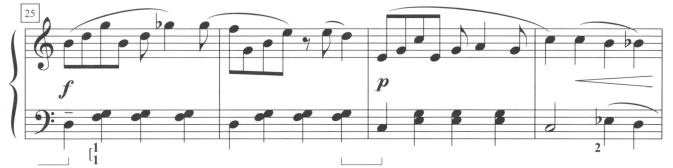

Maple Leaf Rag was written in 1899 by the African-American composer, Scott Joplin. He named the piece after the Maple Leaf Club, a dance hall in Sedalia, Missouri where he worked as a pianist. The music became enormously popular and the profits from music sales enabled him to become a full time composer.

Joplin wanted ragtime to be accepted as a serious musical style and wrote a ragtime ballet and two ragtime operas. Unfortunately, these works were not successful. He remains best known for his ragtime piano solos.

America the Beautiful

Music by Samuel A. Ward
Lyrics by Katherine Lee Bates

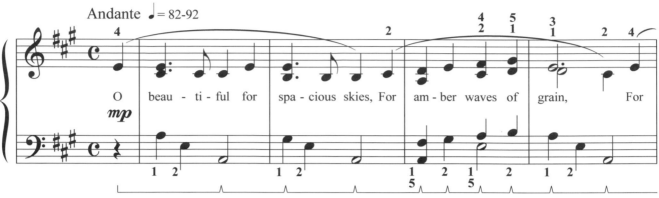

O beau-ti-ful for spa-cious skies, For am-ber waves of grain, For

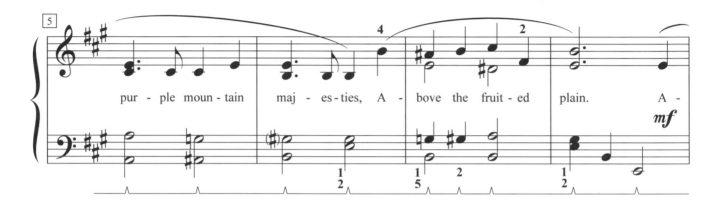

pur - ple moun-tain maj - es - ties, A-bove the fruit-ed plain. A -

mer - i-ca! A - mer - i-ca! God shed His grace on thee, And

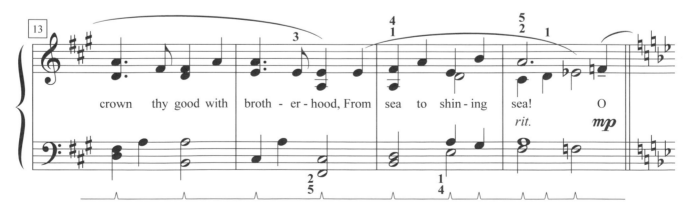

crown thy good with broth-er-hood, From sea to shin-ing sea! O

CD Track 25: Performance tempo
CD Track 26: Practice tempo (played twice)

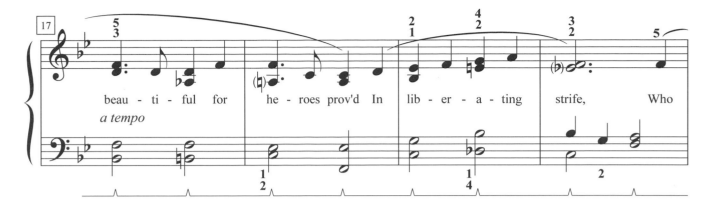

beau - ti - ful for he - roes prov'd In lib - er - a - ting strife, Who

a tempo

more than self their coun - try loved, And mer - cy more than life! A -

mf

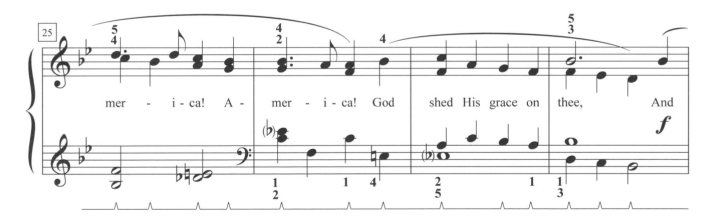

mer - i - ca! A - mer - i - ca! God shed His grace on thee, And

f

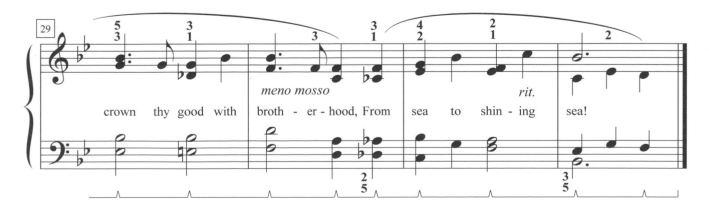

crown thy good with broth - er - hood, From sea to shin - ing sea!

meno mosso   *rit.*

Successful Schaum Sheet Music

• = Original Form ✓ = Chord Symbols